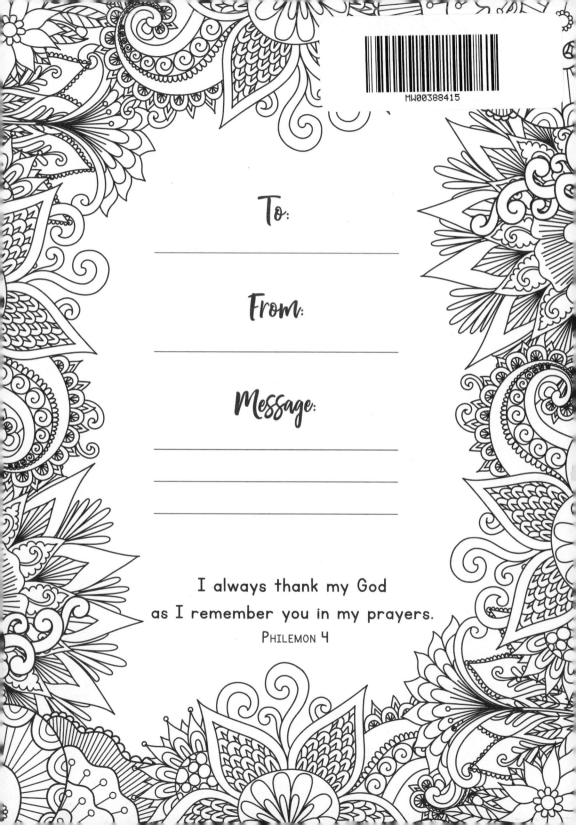

To:

_____

From:

_____

Message:

_____

_____

_____

I always thank my God
as I remember you in my prayers.
PHILEMON 4

Published by Christian Art Publishers
PO Box 1599, Vereeniging, 1930, RSA

© 2022
First edition 2022

Designed by Christian Art Publishers

Cover designed by Christian Art Publishers
Images used under license from Shutterstock.com

Printed in China

ISBN 978-1-4321-3485-3

22 23 24 25 26 27 28 29 30 31 – 10 9 8 7 6 5 4 3 2 1

Pray More Worry Less

CHRISTIAN ART
PUBLISHERS

I praise You, Lord:

DATE:

I am thankful for:

I confess:

I pray for:

If you've made a habit
of communing with God
when the sun is shining,
you'll find it much easier
to sing in the rain.

I praise You, Lord:

DATE:

I am thankful for:

I confess:

I pray for:

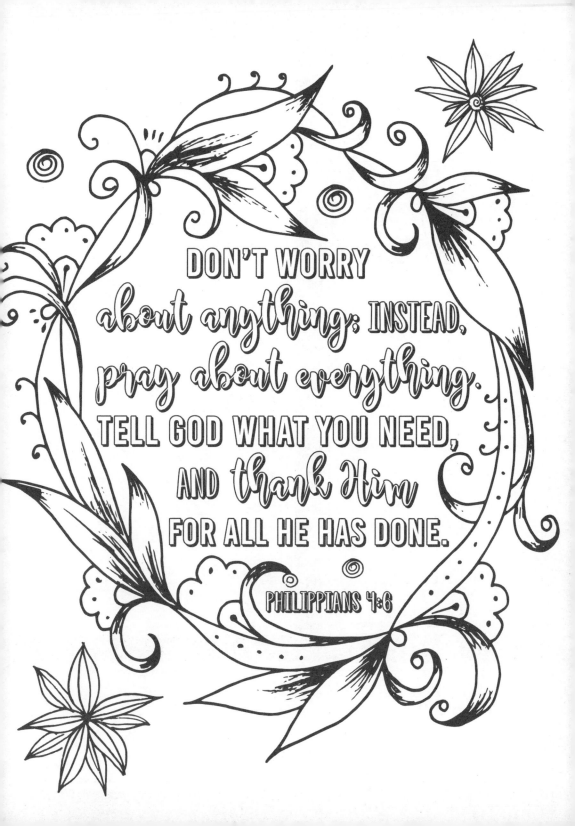

I praise You, Lord:

DATE:

I am thankful for:

I confess:

I pray for:

Grow flowers of gratitude in the soil of prayer.

I praise You, Lord:

DATE:

I am thankful for:

I confess:

I pray for:

REJOICE always, PRAY WITHOUT CEASING, IN EVERYTHING GIVE THANKS; FOR THIS IS THE WILL OF GOD in Christ Jesus FOR YOU.

1 THESSALONIANS 5:16-18

I praise You, Lord:

DATE: _____

I am thankful for:

_____
_____
_____
_____
_____
_____
_____

I confess:

_____
_____
_____
_____
_____
_____

I pray for: _____
_____
_____

As is the business of tailors to make clothes and cobblers to make shoes, so it is the business of Christians to pray. MARTIN LUTHER

I praise You, Lord:

DATE: _____

I am thankful for:

_____
_____
_____
_____
_____
_____
_____
_____
_____
_____
_____

I confess:

_____
_____
_____
_____
_____
_____
_____
_____

I pray for: _____
_____
_____

What is your favorite worship song or hymn about prayer?
Write a stanza or line that stands out for you.
_____

I praise You, Lord:

DATE: _____

I am thankful for:

_____
_____
_____
_____
_____
_____
_____

I confess:

_____
_____
_____
_____
_____
_____

I pray for: _____
_____
_____

IF WE CONFESS OUR SINS,
He is faithful and just
TO FORGIVE US OUR SINS
AND TO *cleanse us*
FROM ALL UNRIGHTEOUSNESS.

1 JOHN 1:9

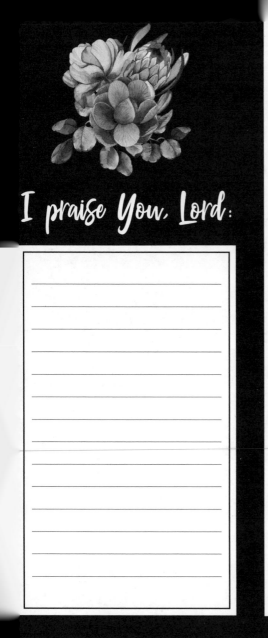

I praise You, Lord:

DATE: _____

I am thankful for:

_____
_____
_____
_____
_____
_____
_____
_____

I confess:

_____
_____
_____
_____
_____
_____
_____

I pray for: _____
_____
_____

Pray the largest prayers.
You cannot think a prayer so large
that God, in answering it, will not
wish you had made it larger.
Pray not for crutches
but for wings.

PHILLIPS BROOKS

I praise You, Lord:

DATE:

I am thankful for:

I confess:

I pray for:

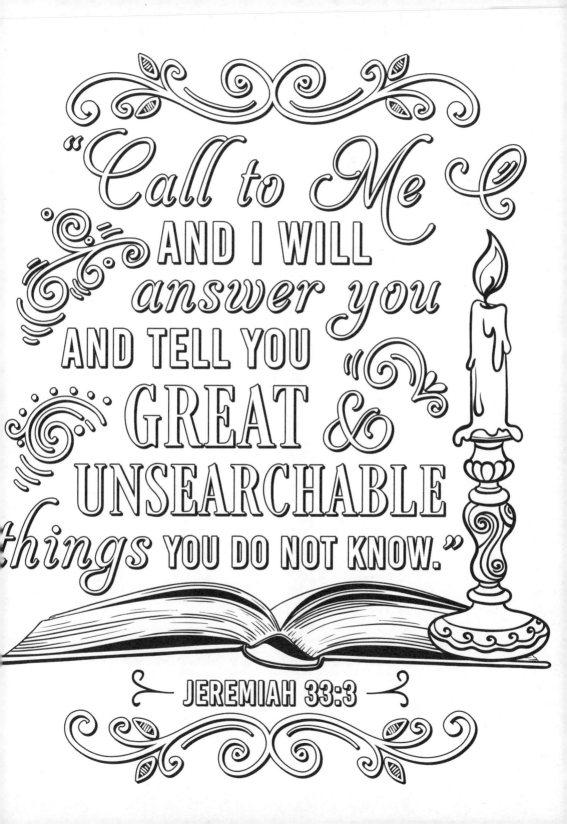

DATE:

I am thankful for:

I praise You, Lord:

I confess:

I pray for:

Let gratitude be the pillow upon which you kneel
to say your prayers at night.

DATE: _____

I am thankful for:

_____
_____
_____
_____
_____
_____
_____

I confess:

_____
_____
_____
_____
_____
_____

I praise You, Lord:

_____
_____
_____
_____
_____
_____
_____
_____
_____
_____

I pray for: _____
_____
_____

DATE:

I am thankful for:

_____
_____
_____
_____
_____
_____
_____

I confess:

_____
_____
_____
_____
_____
_____
_____

I praise You, Lord:

_____
_____
_____
_____
_____
_____
_____
_____
_____
_____
_____

I pray for: _____
_____
_____

PRAYER

Prayer should be the key of the day and the lock of the night. GEORGE HERBERT

I praise You, Lord:

DATE:

I am thankful for:

I confess:

I pray for:

I praise You, Lord:

DATE: _____

I am thankful for:
_____
_____
_____
_____
_____
_____
_____
_____

I confess:
_____
_____
_____
_____
_____
_____

I pray for: _____
_____
_____

It is not well for a person
to pray cream and live skim milk.
HENRY WARD BEECHER

DATE:

I am thankful for:

_____
_____
_____
_____
_____
_____
_____

I confess:

_____
_____
_____
_____
_____
_____

I praise You, Lord:

_____
_____
_____
_____
_____
_____
_____
_____
_____
_____
_____

I pray for: _____
_____
_____

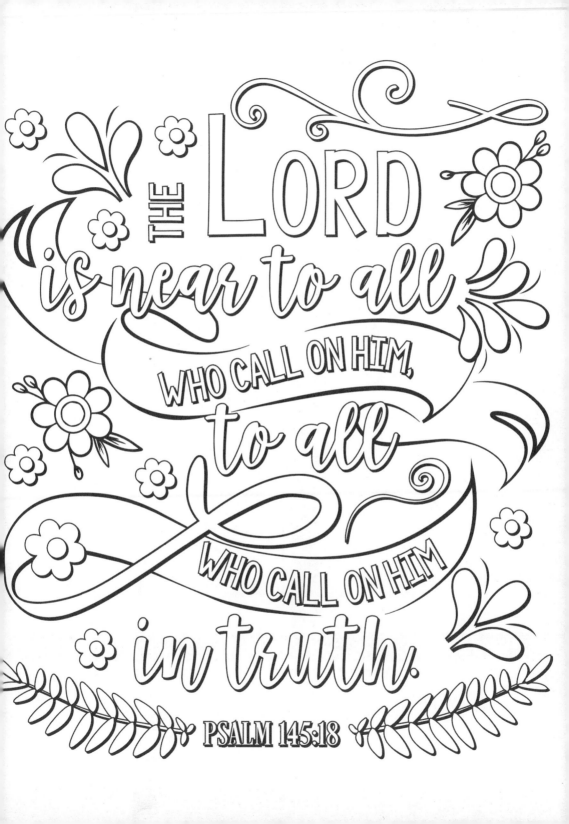

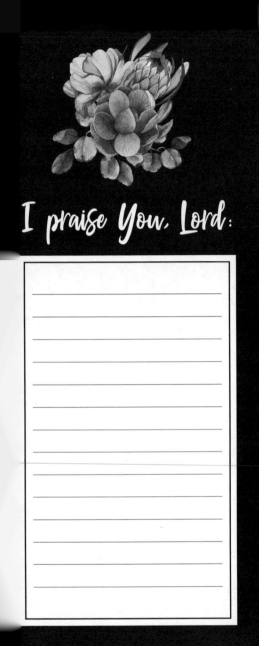

I praise You, Lord:

DATE: _____

I am thankful for:

I confess:

I pray for: _____

Above the storm the smallest prayer will still be heard.

I praise You, Lord:

DATE: _____

I am thankful for:

_____
_____
_____
_____
_____
_____
_____
_____
_____

I confess:

_____
_____
_____
_____
_____
_____
_____
_____

I pray for: _____
_____
_____

Write your favorite Scripture prayer.

I praise You, Lord:

DATE:

I am thankful for:
_____
_____
_____
_____
_____
_____
_____

I confess:
_____
_____
_____
_____
_____
_____

I pray for: _____
_____
_____

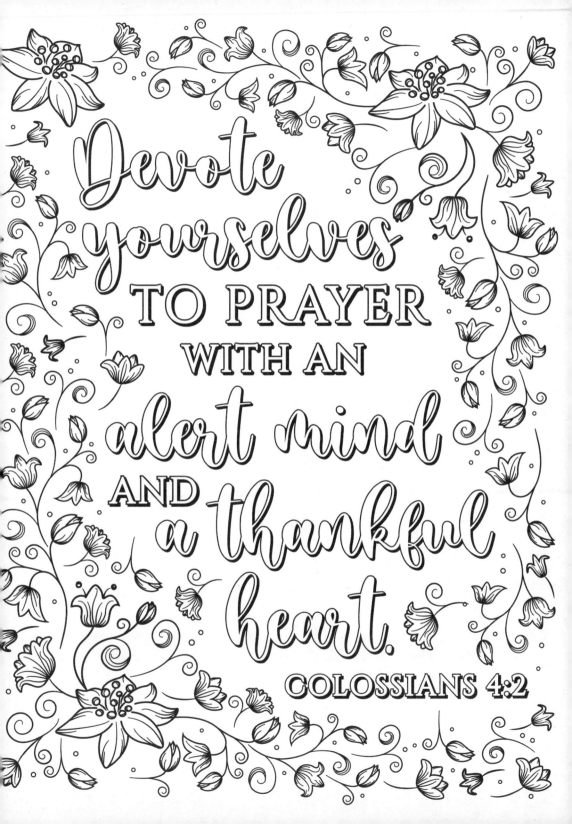

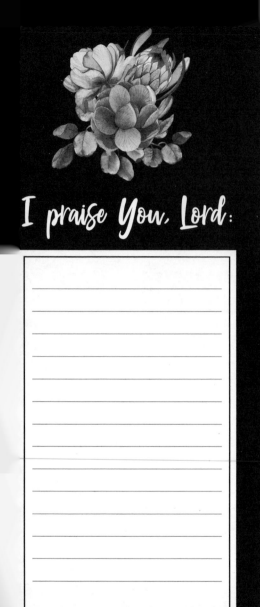

DATE: _____

I am thankful for:

_____
_____
_____
_____
_____
_____
_____
_____

I confess:

_____
_____
_____
_____
_____
_____
_____

I praise You, Lord:

_____
_____
_____
_____
_____
_____
_____
_____
_____

I pray for: _____
_____
_____

The power of prayer
is like turning on a light
as it illuminates
God's purpose
for our lives.

I praise You, Lord:

DATE:

I am thankful for:

I confess:

I pray for:

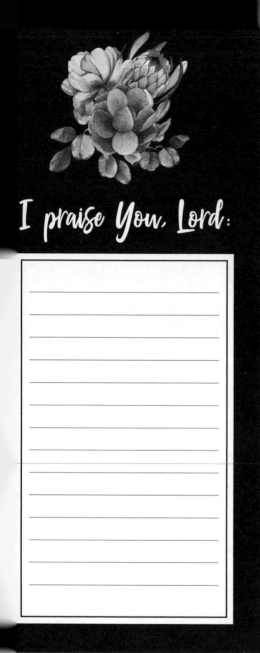

DATE:

I am thankful for:

_____
_____
_____
_____
_____
_____
_____
_____

I confess:

_____
_____
_____
_____
_____

I praise You, Lord:

_____
_____
_____
_____
_____
_____
_____
_____
_____
_____
_____
_____

I pray for: _____
_____
_____

We need to find God, and He cannot be found
in noise and restlessness. God is the friend of silence.
See how nature – trees, flowers, grass – grows in silence;
see the stars, the moon and the sun, how they move in silence.
We need silence to be able to touch souls.
MOTHER TERESA

I praise You, Lord:

DATE: _____

I am thankful for:
_____
_____
_____
_____
_____
_____
_____

I confess:
_____
_____
_____
_____
_____
_____

I pray for: _____
_____
_____

Answer me WHEN I CALL TO YOU, my righteous God. GIVE ME RELIEF FROM MY DISTRESS; have mercy on me & hear MY PRAYER.

PSALM 4:1

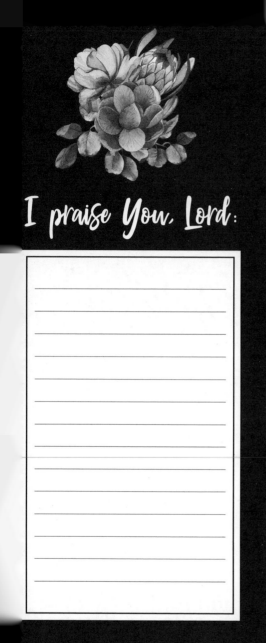

DATE:

I am thankful for:

I confess:

I praise You, Lord:

I pray for:

As well could you expect a plant
to grow without air and water
as to expect your heart to grow
without prayer and faith.
CHARLES SPURGEON

I praise You, Lord:

DATE:

I am thankful for:

_____
_____
_____
_____
_____
_____
_____
_____

I confess:

_____
_____
_____
_____
_____

_____
_____
_____
_____
_____
_____
_____
_____
_____
_____

I pray for: _____
_____
_____

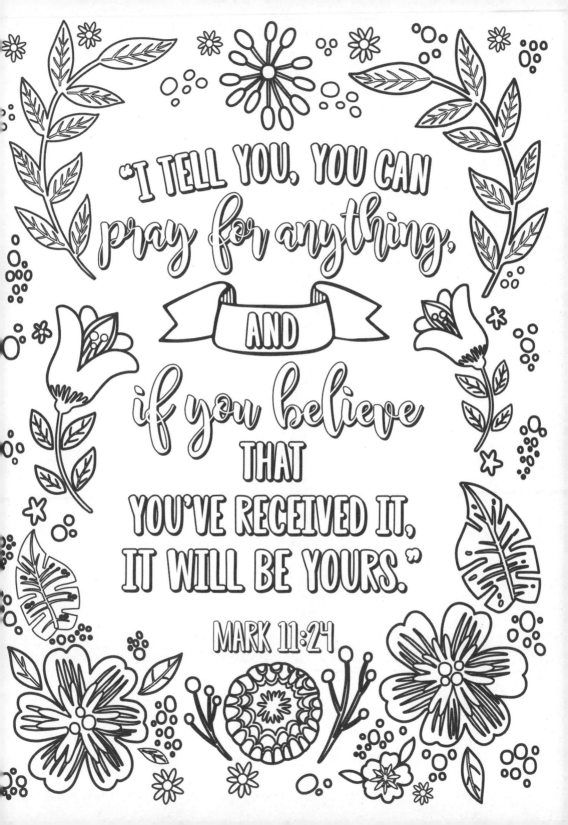

I praise You, Lord:

DATE: _____

I am thankful for:
_____
_____
_____
_____
_____
_____
_____

I confess:
_____
_____
_____
_____
_____
_____
_____

I pray for: _____
_____
_____

Prayer should not be regarded as a duty which must be performed,
but rather as a privilege to be enjoyed,
a rare delight that is always revealing some new beauty.
E. M. BOUNDS

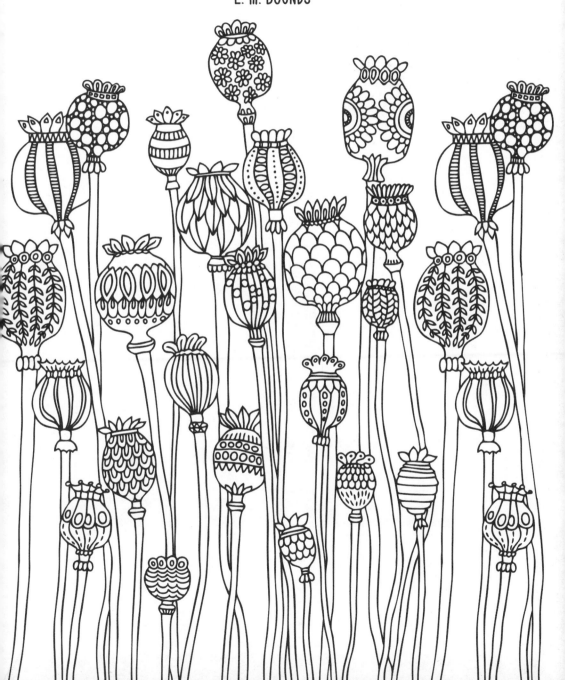

DATE: _____

I am thankful for:
_____
_____
_____
_____
_____
_____
_____
_____

I confess:
_____
_____
_____
_____
_____
_____
_____
_____

I praise You, Lord:
_____
_____
_____
_____
_____
_____
_____
_____
_____
_____
_____

I pray for: _____
_____
_____

Pray in the Spirit AT ALL TIMES AND ON EVERY OCCASION. Stay alert and be persistent IN YOUR PRAYERS FOR ALL BELIEVERS everywhere. EPHESIANS 6:18

DATE:

I am thankful for:

I praise You, Lord:

I confess:

I pray for:

Is prayer your steering wheel
or your spare tire?

CORRIE TEN BOOM

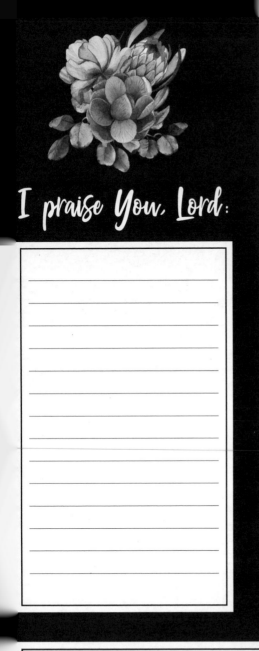

I praise You, Lord:

DATE: _____

I am thankful for:

_____
_____
_____
_____
_____
_____
_____
_____
_____

I confess:

_____
_____
_____
_____
_____
_____
_____

I pray for: _____
_____
_____

Write a prayer of praise to God.
_____

I praise You, Lord:

DATE: _____

I am thankful for:

_____
_____
_____
_____
_____
_____
_____
_____

I confess:

_____
_____
_____
_____
_____
_____
_____

I pray for: _____
_____
_____

LET US COME BOLDLY TO THE THRONE OF our gracious God. THERE WE WILL RECEIVE His mercy, AND WE WILL find grace TO HELP US WHEN WE NEED IT MOST.

HEBREWS 4:16

I praise You, Lord:

DATE:

I am thankful for:

I confess:

I pray for:

Prayer is a strong wall and fortress of the church;
it is a goodly Christian weapon.
MARTIN LUTHER

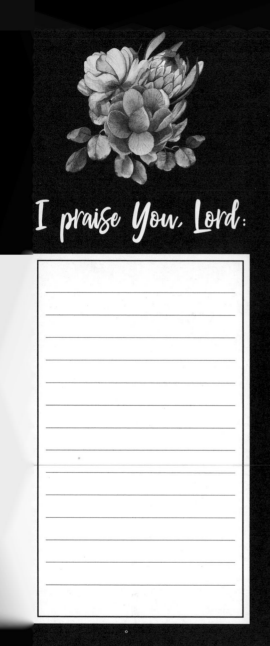

I praise You, Lord:

DATE: _____

I am thankful for:

_____
_____
_____
_____
_____
_____
_____

I confess:

_____
_____
_____
_____
_____
_____

I pray for: _____
_____
_____

THE EYES OF THE LORD *watch over* THOSE WHO DO RIGHT, AND HIS EARS ARE *open to their prayers.*

1 PETER 3:12

I praise You, Lord:

DATE:

I am thankful for:

I confess:

I pray for:

The great thing in prayer is to feel that we are putting
our supplications into the bosom of omnipotent love.
ANDREW MURRAY

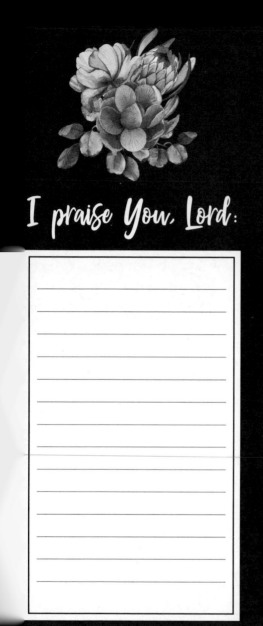

DATE:

I am thankful for:

_____
_____
_____
_____
_____
_____
_____
_____

I confess:

_____
_____
_____
_____
_____
_____
_____
_____

I praise You, Lord:

_____
_____
_____
_____
_____
_____
_____
_____
_____
_____
_____
_____

I pray for: _____
_____
_____

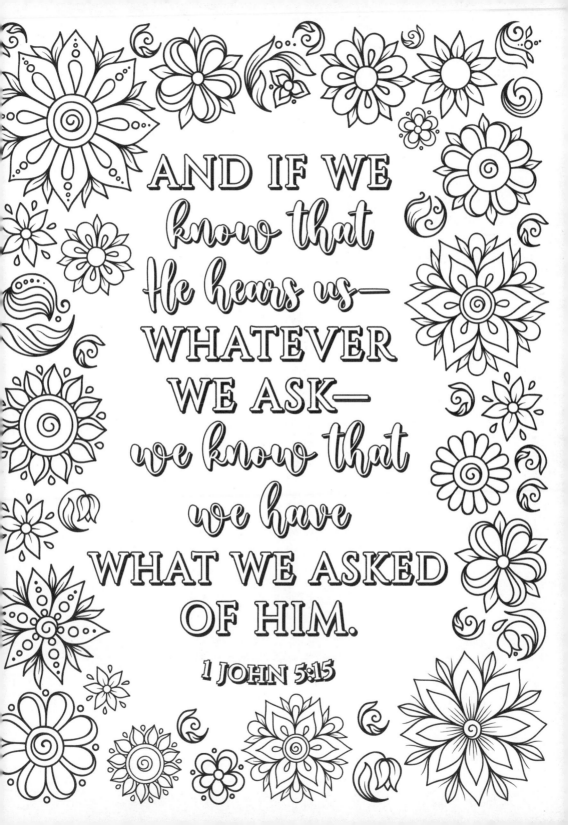

AND IF WE
know that
He hears us—
WHATEVER
WE ASK—
we know that
we have
WHAT WE ASKED
OF HIM.

1 JOHN 5:15

I praise You, Lord:

DATE:

I am thankful for:
_____
_____
_____
_____
_____
_____
_____

I confess:
_____
_____
_____
_____
_____
_____
_____

I pray for: _____
_____
_____

Prayer is the cure for a confused mind,
a weary soul, a sickness, and a broken heart.
No greater peace or contentment
can be achieved than through prayer.

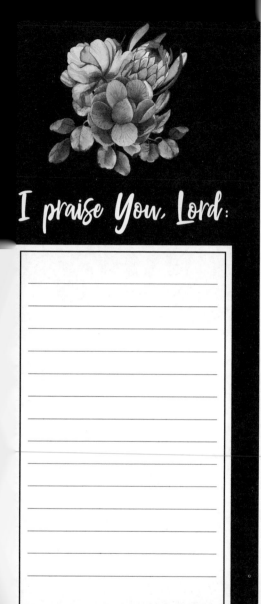

DATE:

I am thankful for:

I confess:

I praise You, Lord:

I pray for:

WHEN YOU ASK, YOU MUST *believe* AND NOT DOUBT, BECAUSE THE ONE WHO DOUBTS IS LIKE *a wave of the sea,* BLOWN AND TOSSED BY THE WIND. JAMES 1:6

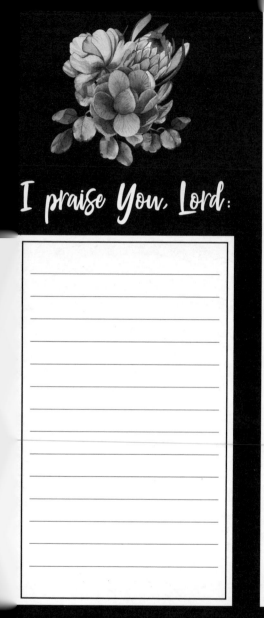

DATE:

I am thankful for:

I praise You, Lord:

I confess:

I pray for:

Walking with God down the avenues of prayer
we acquire something of His likeness,
and unconsciously we become witnesses
to others of His beauty and His grace.

E. M. Bounds

DATE:

I am thankful for:

I praise You, Lord:

I confess:

I pray for:

I praise You, Lord:

DATE: _____

I am thankful for:

_____
_____
_____
_____
_____
_____
_____
_____
_____

I confess:

_____
_____
_____
_____
_____
_____
_____

I pray for: _____
_____
_____

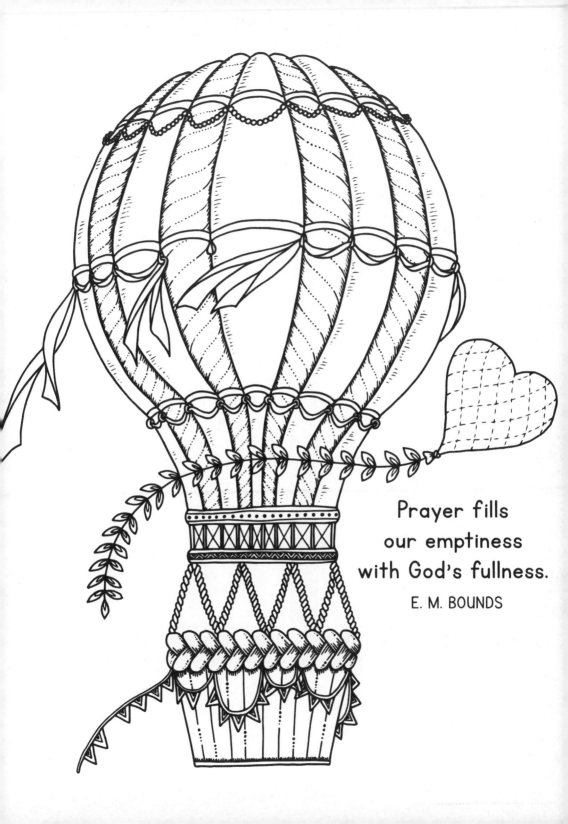

Prayer fills
our emptiness
with God's fullness.

E. M. BOUNDS

DATE:

I am thankful for:

I confess:

I praise You, Lord:

I pray for:

Write the names of your loved ones.
Pray for each one as you letter their name.

DATE: _____

I am thankful for:

_____
_____
_____
_____
_____
_____
_____
_____

I confess:

_____
_____
_____
_____
_____
_____
_____
_____

I praise You, Lord:

_____
_____
_____
_____
_____
_____
_____
_____
_____
_____
_____

I pray for: _____
_____
_____

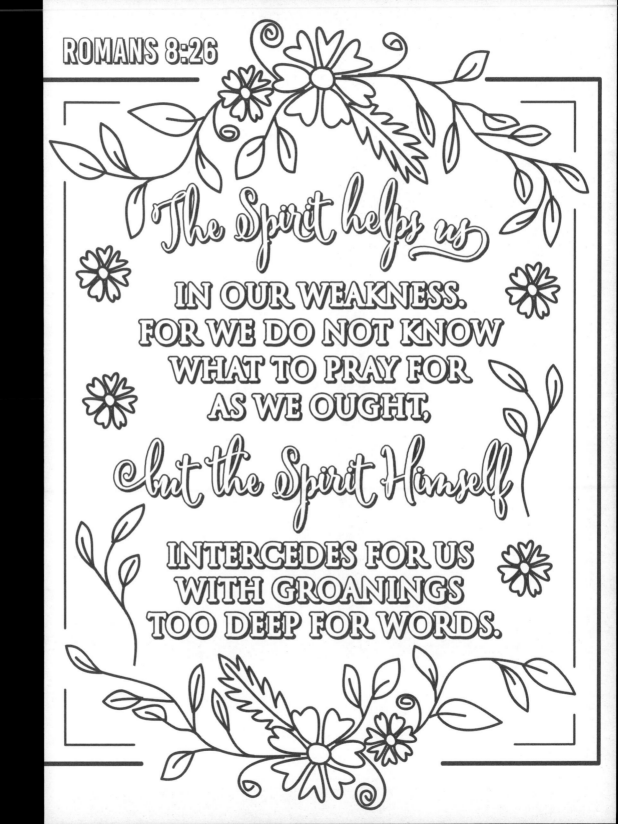

ROMANS 8:26

The Spirit helps us
IN OUR WEAKNESS.
FOR WE DO NOT KNOW
WHAT TO PRAY FOR
AS WE OUGHT,
but the Spirit Himself
INTERCEDES FOR US
WITH GROANINGS
TOO DEEP FOR WORDS.

I praise You, Lord:

DATE:

I am thankful for:

I confess:

I pray for:

The sweetest time of the day is when you pray.
Because you are talking to the One who loves you the most.

I praise You, Lord:

DATE:

I am thankful for:

I confess:

I pray for:

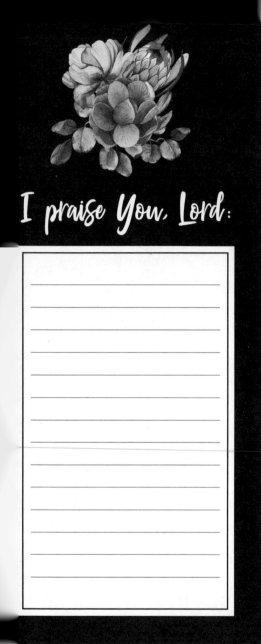

I praise You, Lord:

DATE: _____

I am thankful for:

_____
_____
_____
_____
_____
_____
_____
_____

I confess:

_____
_____
_____
_____
_____
_____
_____

I pray for: _____
_____
_____

Prayer is the key that unlocks all the storehouses of God's infinite grace and power.

R. A. TORREY

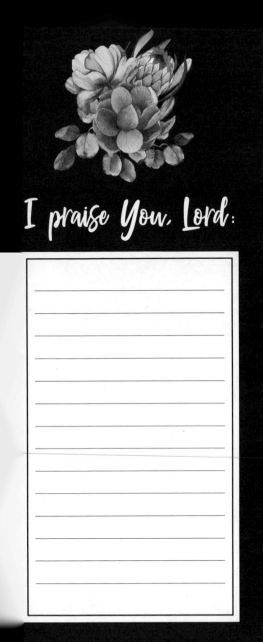

DATE:

I am thankful for:

_____
_____
_____
_____
_____
_____
_____
_____

I confess:

_____
_____
_____
_____
_____
_____
_____

I praise You, Lord:

_____
_____
_____
_____
_____
_____
_____
_____
_____
_____
_____

I pray for: _____
_____
_____

"AND WHEN YOU stand praying, IF YOU HOLD ANYTHING AGAINST ANYONE, forgive them, SO THAT your Father in heaven MAY FORGIVE YOU YOUR SINS."

MARK 11:25

I praise You, Lord:

DATE:

I am thankful for:

_____
_____
_____
_____
_____
_____
_____
_____
_____

I confess:

_____
_____
_____
_____
_____
_____
_____
_____
_____
_____
_____
_____

I pray for: _____
_____
_____

Prayer is the thread that links us to God.
Through prayer many broken hearts have been mended.

I praise You, Lord:

DATE: _____

I am thankful for:

_____
_____
_____
_____
_____
_____
_____
_____

I confess:

_____
_____
_____
_____
_____
_____

I pray for: _____
_____
_____

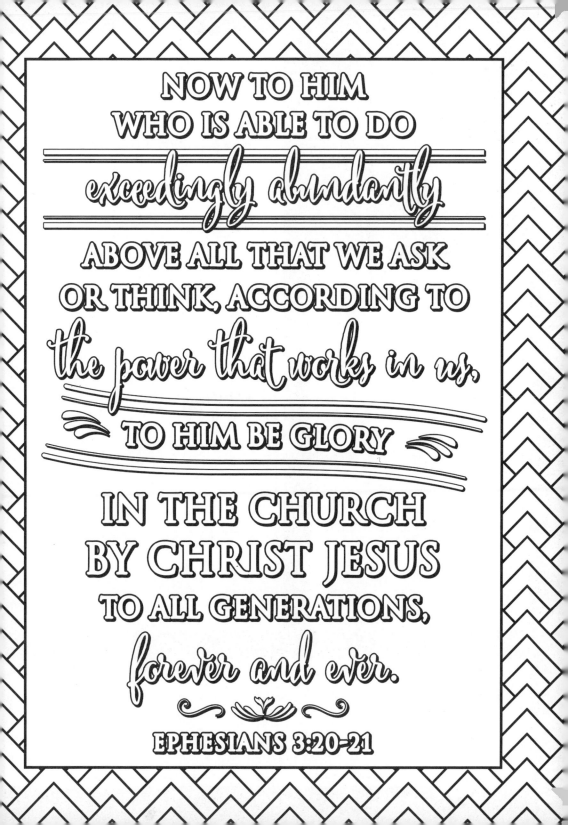

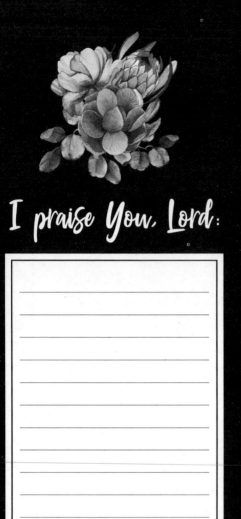

I praise You, Lord:

DATE:

I am thankful for:

I confess:

I pray for:

He who kneels the most, stands the best.
D. L. MOODY

DATE: _____

I am thankful for:

_____
_____
_____
_____
_____
_____
_____
_____

I confess:

_____
_____
_____
_____
_____
_____
_____

I praise You, Lord:

_____
_____
_____
_____
_____
_____
_____
_____
_____
_____

I pray for: _____
_____
_____

AND WHATEVER WE ASK *we receive from Him,* BECAUSE WE KEEP HIS COMMANDMENTS AND DO THOSE THINGS THAT ARE *pleasing in His sight*

1 JOHN 3:22

I praise You, Lord:

DATE: _____

I am thankful for:

_____
_____
_____
_____
_____
_____
_____
_____
_____

I confess:

_____
_____
_____
_____
_____
_____
_____

I pray for: _____
_____
_____

O, let the place
of secret prayer
become to me the
most beloved spot
on earth.
ANDREW MURRAY

I praise You, Lord:

DATE: _____

I am thankful for:
_____
_____
_____
_____
_____
_____
_____
_____

I confess:
_____
_____
_____
_____
_____
_____
_____
_____

I pray for: _____
_____
_____

List 5 things you are grateful to God for.

I praise You, Lord:

DATE: _____

I am thankful for:

_____
_____
_____
_____
_____
_____
_____
_____

I confess:

_____
_____
_____
_____
_____
_____

I pray for: _____
_____
_____

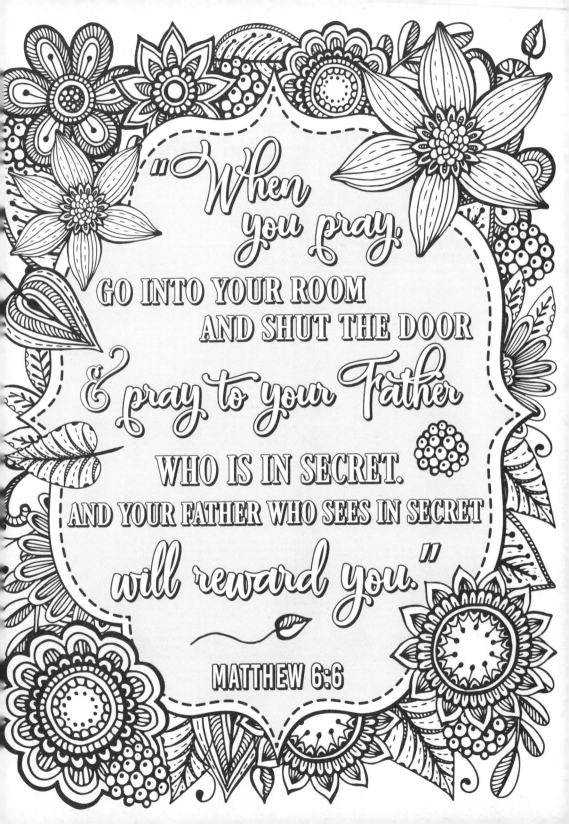

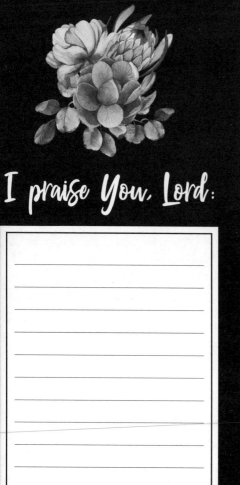

DATE:

I am thankful for:

I praise You, Lord:

I confess:

I pray for:

God is fighting your battles, arranging things in your favor, and making a way even when you don't see a way.

I praise You, Lord:

DATE:

I am thankful for:

I confess:

I pray for:

DATE: _____

I am thankful for:

_____
_____
_____
_____
_____
_____
_____

I confess:

_____
_____
_____
_____
_____
_____

I praise You, Lord:

_____
_____
_____
_____
_____
_____
_____
_____
_____
_____
_____
_____

I pray for: _____
_____
_____

God cares about the
finest details of your life.
No burden is too small
or care too light to be carried
on the wings of prayer.

I praise You, Lord:

DATE: _____

I am thankful for:

_____
_____
_____
_____
_____
_____
_____

I confess:

_____
_____
_____
_____
_____
_____
_____

I pray for: _____
_____
_____

SEEK THE LORD & His strength; SEEK HIS PRESENCE continually!

1 CHRONICLES 16:11

I praise You, Lord:

DATE: _____

I am thankful for:
_____
_____
_____
_____
_____
_____
_____

I confess:
_____
_____
_____
_____
_____
_____

I pray for: _____
_____
_____

Write John 3:16 and thank God for your salvation.
_____

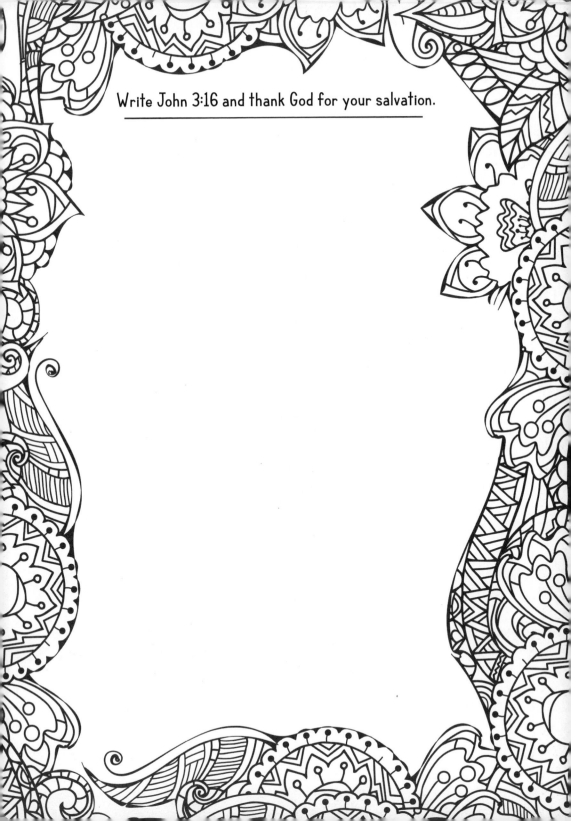

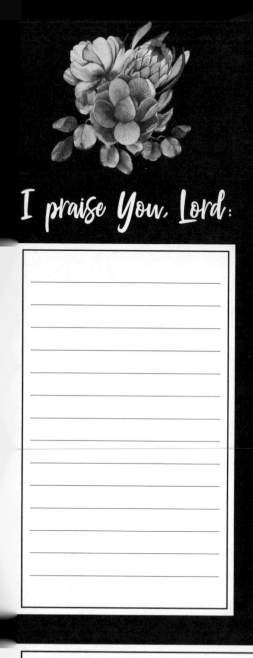

I praise You, Lord:

DATE: _____

I am thankful for:
_____
_____
_____
_____
_____
_____
_____
_____

I confess:
_____
_____
_____
_____
_____
_____
_____

I pray for: _____
_____
_____

The best and sweetest flowers of paradise
God gives to His people when they are upon their knees.
Prayer is the gate of heaven.

THOMAS BROOKS

I praise You, Lord:

DATE:

I am thankful for:

I confess:

I pray for:

THE LORD
hears His people
WHEN THEY CALL
TO HIM FOR HELP.
He rescues
THEM FROM
ALL THEIR TROUBLES.

PSALM 34:17

I praise You, Lord:

DATE: _____

I am thankful for:
_____
_____
_____
_____
_____
_____
_____
_____

I confess:
_____
_____
_____
_____
_____
_____

I pray for: _____
_____
_____

If your day is hemmed in with prayer,
it is less likely to come unraveled.

CYNTHIA LEWIS

DATE: _____

I am thankful for:

_____
_____
_____
_____
_____
_____
_____
_____
_____
_____

I confess:

_____
_____
_____
_____
_____
_____
_____
_____
_____

I praise You, Lord:

_____
_____
_____
_____
_____
_____
_____
_____
_____
_____
_____

I pray for: _____

_____
_____

DATE:

I am thankful for:

_____
_____
_____
_____
_____
_____
_____

I confess:

_____
_____
_____
_____
_____
_____

I praise You, Lord:

_____
_____
_____
_____
_____
_____
_____
_____
_____
_____
_____
_____

I pray for: _____
_____
_____

DATE:

I am thankful for:

I confess:

I praise You, Lord:

I pray for:

List some of the names of God
and thank Him for these qualities.

_____